J   4556931H
523.3   Asimov, Isaac, 1920-
ASI   The moon

 W9-AQK-678

HICKORY FLAT PUBLIC LIBRARY
2740 EAST CHEROKEE DRIVE
CANTON, GEORGIA 30115

SEQUOYAH REGIONAL LIBRARY

3 8749 0045 5693 1

Isaac Asimov's
21st Century
Library of the
Universe

The Solar System

The Moon

BY ISAAC ASIMOV
WITH REVISIONS AND UPDATING BY RICHARD HANTULA

THIS BOOK IS THE PROPERTY OF
SEQUOYAH REGIONAL LIBRARY
CANTON, GEORGIA

Gareth Stevens Publishing
A WORLD ALMANAC EDUCATION GROUP COMPANY

Please visit our web site at: **www.garethstevens.com**
For a free color catalog describing Gareth Stevens Publishing's list of high-quality
books and multimedia programs, call 1-800-542-2595 (USA) or 1-800-387-3178 (Canada).
Gareth Stevens Publishing's fax: (414) 332-3567.

The reproduction rights to all photographs and illustrations in this book are controlled by the individuals
or institutions credited on page 32 and may not be reproduced without their permission.

Library of Congress Cataloging-In-Publication Data

Asimov, Isaac.
    The moon / by Isaac Asimov; with revisions and updating by Richard Hantula.
       p. cm. — (Isaac Asimov's 21st century library of the universe. The solar system)
    Rev. ed. of: The moon. 1994.
    Summary: Examines the many facets and puzzles of our Moon, including its phases and eclipses,
its early discoveries and modern exploration, and its possible origins and future prospects.
    Includes bibliographical references and index.
    ISBN 0-8368-3238-8 (lib. bdg.)
    1. Moon—Juvenile literature. [1. Moon.] I. Hantula, Richard. II. Asimov, Isaac. The moon.
III. Title. IV. Isaac Asimov's 21st century library of the universe. Solar system.
QB582.A85 2002
523.3—dc21   2002066920

This edition first published in 2002 by
Gareth Stevens Publishing
A World Almanac Education Group Company
330 West Olive Street, Suite 100
Milwaukee, WI 53212 USA

Revised and updated edition © 2002 by Gareth Stevens, Inc. Original edition published in 1988
by Gareth Stevens, Inc. under the title *The Earth's Moon*. Second edition published in 1994 by
Gareth Stevens, Inc. under the title *The Moon*. Text © 2002 by Nightfall, Inc. End matter and
revisions © 2002 by Gareth Stevens, Inc.

Series editor: Betsy Rasmussen
Cover design and layout adaptation: Melissa Valuch
Production director: Susan Ashley
Picture research: Kathy Keller
Additional picture research: Diane Laska-Swanke
Artwork commissioning: Kathy Keller and Laurie Shock

The editors at Gareth Stevens Publishing have selected science author Richard Hantula to bring
this classic series of young people's information books up to date. Richard Hantula has written
and edited books and articles on science and technology for more than two decades. He was
the senior U.S. editor for the *Macmillan Encyclopedia of Science*.

In addition to Hantula's contribution to this most recent edition, the editors would like to
acknowledge the participation of two noted science authors, Greg Walz-Chojnacki and
Francis Reddy, as contributors to earlier editions of this work.

All rights to this edition reserved to Gareth Stevens, Inc. No part of this book may be reproduced,
stored in a retrieval system, or transmitted in any form or by any means, electronic, mechanical,
photocopying, recording, or otherwise without the prior written permission of the publisher except
for the inclusion of brief quotations in an acknowledged review.

Printed in the United States of America

1 2 3 4 5 6 7 8 9 06 05 04 03 02

Contents

Ruler of the Night Sky 4
A Closer Look 6
An Ever-Changing Moon 8
Now You See It, Now You Don't 10
A Double Planet 12
Moon Travel 14
The First Step on the Moon 15
Coming Back to the Moon 16
Origins of the Moon 18
Cosmic Collision 20
A Different World 22
Lunar Life 24
A New Home Base 26
Craters on the Moon 28

More Books about the Moon 30
CD-ROMs and DVDs 30
Web Sites 30
Places to Visit 30
Glossary 31
Index 32

• The Moon •

We live in an enormously large place – the Universe. It is only natural that we would want to understand this place, so scientists and engineers have developed instruments and spacecrafts that have told us far more about the Universe than we could possibly imagine.

We have seen planets up close, and spacecrafts have even landed on some. We have learned about quasars and pulsars, super-novas and colliding galaxies, and black holes and dark matter. We have gathered amazing data about how the Universe may have come into being and how it may end. Nothing could be more astonishing.

Our Moon is about 238,900 miles (384,400 kilometers) away from Earth, on average. The next nearest sizable object in space is the planet Venus. Even when it is at its closest, Venus is still about 100 times as far away as the Moon. Mars is about 140 times as far away at its closest. All the other worlds in our Solar System are much, much farther. In fact, the Moon is only three days away by rocket ship, and it is the only world other than Earth that humans have stood upon.

Ruler of the Night Sky

There is no doubt about it — the Moon is the ruler of our night sky. Aside from comets, which do not occur very often, everything else in the night sky is just a point of light. The Moon, however, is large enough and close enough to give us light at night. It is close enough for its gravitational pull to drag our seas upward and cause the tides. We can see both shadows and bright spots on the Moon's surface. These shadows and bright spots have played games with people's eyes for thousands of years. Long ago, people thought the shadows might be a person. That is why we have all heard about "the man in the Moon," even though there is no such thing. Not so long ago, some people thought the Moon was a world like Earth. Of course we now know this is not true. Even in ancient times, tales about trips to the Moon existed. Thanks to our modern science and our old-fashioned curiosity, these tales have come true.

Left: Over the years, people have seen many faces in the Moon's surface. This is how one artist imagines the Moon looks when only $1/4$ of its surface is revealed by sunlight.

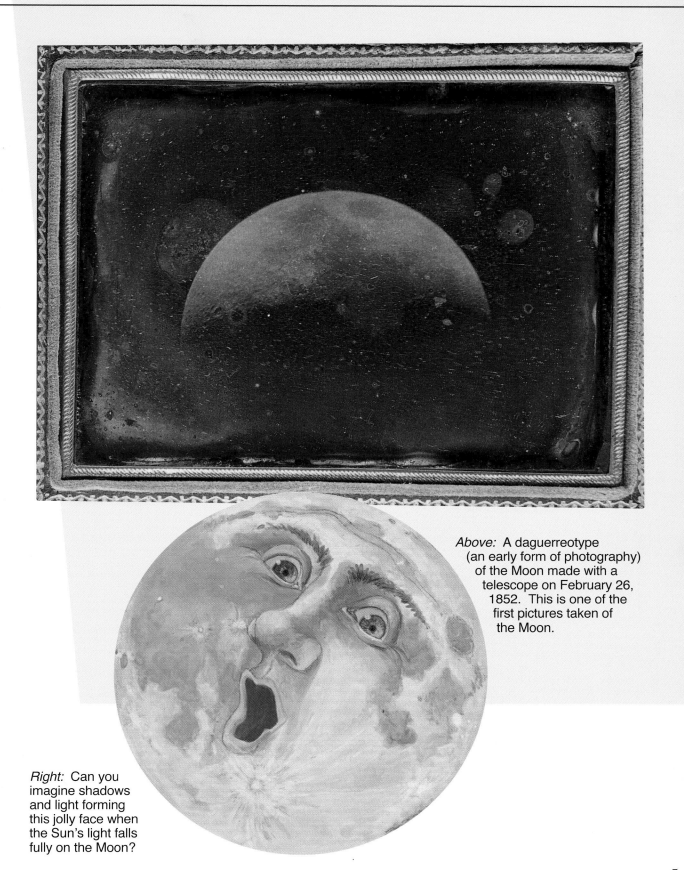

Above: A daguerreotype (an early form of photography) of the Moon made with a telescope on February 26, 1852. This is one of the first pictures taken of the Moon.

Right: Can you imagine shadows and light forming this jolly face when the Sun's light falls fully on the Moon?

A Closer Look

In ancient times, people looked at the Moon with only their eyes. Then, in 1609, an Italian scientist named Galileo Galilei built a telescope that made objects in space look larger and nearer. The first object he looked at was the Moon. He saw mountain ranges and craters through the telescope. A few craters had bright streaks coming out all around them. The shadows on the Moon turned out to be flat dark areas. Galileo thought they might be seas of water, and they are still sometimes called *maria*, from the Latin word for "sea." It turned out that they were not seas, however, because there is no liquid water on the Moon. Also, there is almost no atmosphere.

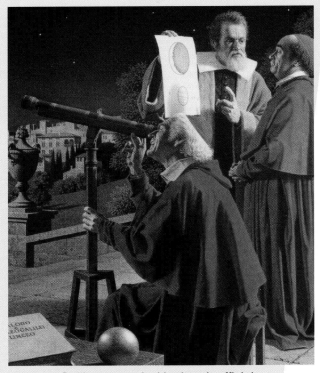

Above: Galileo argued with church officials over his ideas. What Galileo saw through his telescope was very different from what was generally believed to be true.

The Moon's craters — look out above!

Some craters on the Moon may be a result of volcanic action, but most were caused by meteorites bombarding the Moon's surface. Most of these strikes occurred in the early days of the Moon, but some may have happened in more recent times. On June 25, 1178, five monks in Canterbury, England, recorded that "a flaming torch sprang up, spewing out fire, hot coals, and sparks" from the edge of the Moon. Scientists think that a meteorite must have struck the Moon just at the edge of the far side. There is simply no way of predicting when a large object might strike the Moon — or Earth.

Above: A photograph of the Moon taken in 1960. Imagine Galileo's surprise at seeing this surface through his telescope.

Left: The crater Langrenus. To cross the crater, you would have to walk about 85 miles (137 kilometers). This is how Langrenus looked on December 24, 1968, from the *Apollo 8* spacecraft orbiting the Moon.

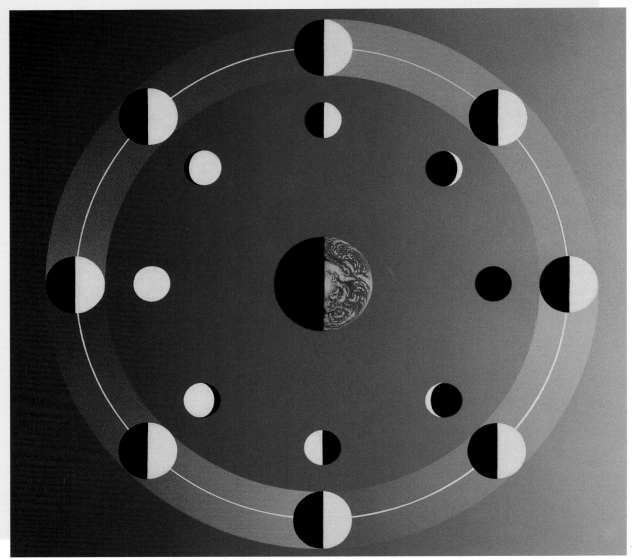

Above: Images of the Moon reflecting sunlight as it circles Earth. The inner circle shows the phases of the Moon viewed from Earth as sunlight is reflected from the Moon's surface. The outer circle shows the Moon from a point in space high above our North Pole. From there, the Moon does not seem to go through phases at all.

| New (or Crescent) Moon | First Quarter | Gibbous Moon Waxing | Full Moon | Gibbous Moon Waning | Last Quarter | Old Moon |

Above: The phases of the Moon as seen from Earth.

An Ever-Changing Moon

Is moonlight really light that is made by the Moon? We know that it is not. The light we see when we look at the Moon is sunlight that shines on the Moon's surface and is reflected back into space. The Moon moves in its orbit around Earth, and, as it does, different parts of it are lit by the Sun. When the Moon and Sun are on opposite sides of Earth, the side of the moon we see is lit. We call this view the full Moon. When the Moon is between Earth and the Sun, the side of the Moon that is lit is away from us and we do not see the Moon. Other times, the Moon is partly lit. It goes from full Moon to full Moon in about a month's time. Long ago, people used the Moon as a calendar.

Below: Tides are caused by the pull of the Moon's gravity on Earth's surfaces. Land is too firm to respond noticeably to the pull, but water stretches toward and away from the Moon. In this diagram, the light blue, egg-shaped areas give an idea of how the tides rise and fall around the world as the Moon orbits Earth. (The diagram exaggerates the size of the tides to make it easier to see them.)

Above: A solar eclipse, in which the Moon blocks the Sun's light from part of Earth. The area on Earth within the smaller circle sees a total eclipse, in which the sky becomes quite dark. The area between the smaller circle and the outer circle has a "shadowy" partial eclipse.

Above: During a lunar eclipse, Earth is between the Moon and the Sun and casts its shadow on the bright side of the Moon.

Now You See It, Now You Don't

Usually, when the Moon approaches the Sun's position in the sky, it goes a little bit above or below the Sun. Sometimes, though, it cuts right across the Sun's position and hides it for a while. This is called a solar eclipse, and it only lasts a few minutes. On the other hand, sometimes when the Moon is full (on the opposite side of Earth from the Sun), it passes through the shadow Earth creates. When Earth's shadow falls on the bright side of the Moon, it makes the Moon's surface dark. This is called a lunar eclipse, and it can last up to a couple of hours.

It is okay to watch an eclipse of the Moon, but you must never directly watch an eclipse of the Sun. Staring into the Sun can hurt your eyes very badly.

Below: This photo was taken from Earth during a total solar eclipse. It gives a spectacular view of the Sun's corona.

Above: A lunar eclipse as it is happening. If you are on the night side of Earth during a lunar eclipse, you will be able to see the effects on the Moon as it slowly slides into Earth's shadow.

A Double Planet

The Moon is quite large. It is 2,159 miles (3,475 km) in diameter (a little over $^1/4$ as wide as Earth). The Moon's surface is nearly as large as North and South America put together. The Moon is not the only big satellite in our Solar System. Jupiter has four big satellites, three of them larger than our Moon. Saturn also has a satellite larger than our Moon. Jupiter and Saturn, however, are giant planets. It is amazing that a planet as small as Earth should have so large a satellite. Considering how small Earth is and how large the Moon is, the Earth and Moon together are almost a double planet.

This picture, taken by the space probe *Galileo* in 1992, shows the "double planet" Earth-Moon. It shows the far side of the Moon, the side we cannot see from Earth. The picture was taken from 3.9 million miles (6.2 million km) away.

Above: Compared to other natural satellites in the Solar System, our Moon is so big that we might ask whether Earth is the Moon's partner rather than its parent. This photo was taken on the *Apollo 8* mission. It dramatically shows Earth on the Moon's horizon.

Will the real double planet please stand up?

The Moon is only about $1/80$ as massive as Earth. Still, most other satellites in the Solar System have less than $1/1{,}000$ of the mass of their parent planet. That is why the combination of Earth and the Moon is considered to be a kind of double planet. In our Solar System, the only other "double planet" is the combination of the distant planet Pluto and its satellite Charon. Pluto is smaller than Earth's Moon. Charon is smaller still, but it is $1/8$ the size of Pluto. Also, Charon is so near to Pluto, that some astronomers think the two may even share the same atmosphere! So Pluto-Charon is closer to being a double planet than is Earth-Moon.

13

Moon Travel

We Earthlings have never been happy just to sit and stare at the Moon. Almost as soon as we began sending rockets into outer space in the 1950s, we aimed them in the direction of the Moon. In 1959, the former Soviet Union landed a probe named *Luna 2* on the Moon. A little later that year, it sent a probe called *Luna 3* around the Moon. *Luna 3* took the first pictures of the far side of the Moon, which we never see from Earth. Spacecrafts from the United States soon joined the Soviet probes. Lunar orbiters photographed all parts of the Moon closely. Scientists were looking for a place for humans to land.

Above: Luna 3 probe. This research spacecraft, launched by the former Soviet Union in 1959, produced the first photographs of the far side of the Moon.

Above: The far side of the Moon. The crew of the U.S. spacecraft *Apollo 13* took this photograph. The large lunar "sea," called Mare Moscoviense after the Russian city of Moscow, can be seen in the upper right area of this picture.

Above: A view of the same area as that pictured left. The large crater on the horizon has the name International Astronomical Union Crater No. 221.

The First Step on the Moon

Eventually, the former Soviet Union and the United States began to send people into space. These people are called astronauts in the United States and cosmonauts in Russia. The United States decided to send astronauts to the Moon. During the 1960s, many test missions were flown. On July 20, 1969, the big moment arrived.

Neil Armstrong stepped off the *Apollo 11* lunar lander and became the first human to walk on another world. After that, U.S. astronauts made five more landings on the Moon. They ran experiments there and brought back Moon rocks for scientists to study. These rocks gave us a chance to look at the Moon in a completely new way.

Left: With no wind on the Moon to blow it away, U.S. astronaut Buzz Aldrin's footprint could remain as it is shown here for billions of years.

Above: Alan L. Bean, pilot for the U.S. *Apollo 12* mission, gathers lunar soil for research in 1969. Also seen in this photo is Charles Conrad, Jr., who is reflected in Bean's helmet.

Left: The U.S. flag, held in a permanent wave by its wire frame, adds a dash of color to the moonscape. *Apollo 15* astronaut Jim Irwin salutes.

Coming Back to the Moon

Although probes were sent to Venus, Mars, Jupiter, and beyond, the 1976 Soviet unmanned probe *Luna 24* was the last spacecraft to visit the Moon for many years. That changed in the 1990s as three U.S. probes explored the Moon, taking new pictures and looking at its surface with advanced instruments. *Galileo*, following a roundabout path to Jupiter, passed by the Moon in 1990 and 1992. *Clementine* orbited the Moon for a few months in 1994, and *Lunar Prospector* was placed in orbit around the Moon in 1998. Both *Clementine* and *Lunar Prospector* found evidence suggesting that water, in the form of ice, might exist on the Moon. This is important because water is something that people will need if they decide to live there. Unfortunately, when *Lunar Prospector* crashed on the Moon in 1999, scientists failed to detect any signs of water in the debris that it raised, but that did not disprove the possibility of water existing on the Moon.

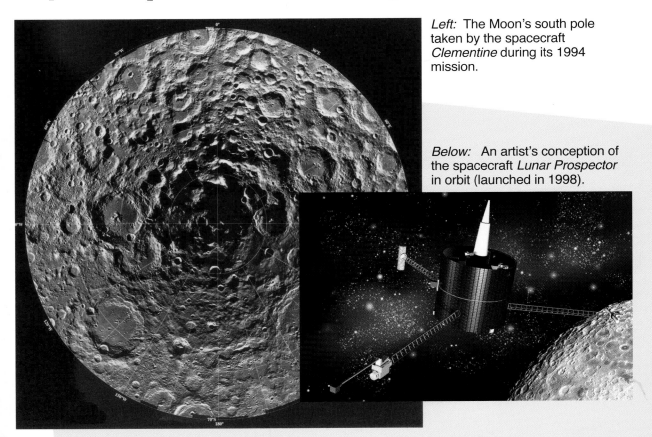

Left: The Moon's south pole taken by the spacecraft *Clementine* during its 1994 mission.

Below: An artist's conception of the spacecraft *Lunar Prospector* in orbit (launched in 1998).

A computer made this color image of the Moon from 53 pictures taken by the spacecraft *Galileo* in 1992. The computer gave different colors to different kinds of rocks. The study of Moon rocks helps scientists understand the Moon's history.

17

Above: An artist's idea of how the Moon might have looked not long after it was formed. It was then much closer to Earth than it is today. A ring of leftover debris accompanies the Moon in its orbit around Earth.

Right: An electron microscope view of lunar dust collected by the U.S. *Apollo 16* mission.

Origins of the Moon

After all the early visits to the Moon by probes, scientists knew more about our Moon than ever before. The Moon's origins, however, were still a mystery, and scientists could not say for sure why Earth had such a large moon. One theory was that when Earth was formed, it spun so fast that a large piece of it split off. In actuality, though, Earth never spun fast enough for this to happen. Perhaps the Moon was an independent planet, and it was trapped by Earth's gravitational force when it passed too closely. That did not seem likely, either. Maybe when Earth was formed, two worlds were formed. In that case, Earth and the Moon should be made of the same materials, but Moon rocks showed this was not so.

Above: Moon rocks brought back by the *Apollo 11* mission.

The mystery of our two-faced Moon

One side of the Moon always faces us. The other side always faces away. Once the Soviets and Americans had photographed the far side, scientists discovered that the two sides were quite different. The side that faces us contains most of the flat dark areas we call maria, or seas (even though there is no water in them). The far side has only a few small seas but far more small craters than the near side. Perhaps meteorite strikes — the main cause for the creation of craters — occurred at different rates on each side of the Moon. If so, why? Scientists are not sure.

Cosmic Collision

After years of studying lunar rocks, most scientists came to a belief about what happened when Earth and other worlds were created. A world, perhaps the size of Mars or even larger, collided with Earth, hitting it a glancing blow and knocking pieces off of it. Scientists have devised computer programs that show what may have happened if such a world did hit Earth. The results suggest that an object like the Moon could have formed out of Earth's outer layers but without Earth's inner layers. Also, the Moon may have received some material from the world that hit Earth. Ideas like these could explain why the Moon does not have the same makeup as Earth.

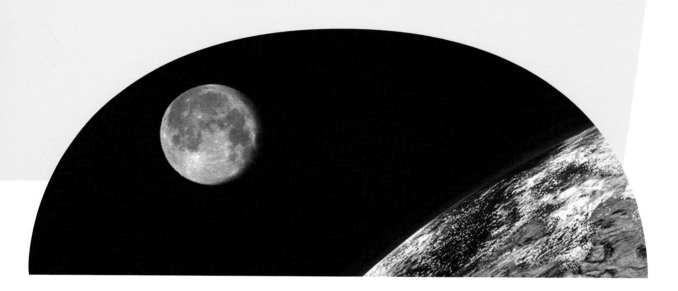

Lunar time vs. solar time

Ancient people who used the Moon for a calendar measured their years in "lunar" time, which would be twelve new moons from one spring to the next. That was not quite enough to fill a whole year — the time it takes for Earth to travel once around the Sun. So every couple of years, they would add a month and count thirteen new moons to the year. Later, certain cultures decided it was easier to make the months a bit longer so that there were always twelve months to a year. The date of Easter is still based on the old lunar calendar. That is why it keeps changing dates from year to year. Muslims use a lunar calendar with twelve months in a year. Their calendar year is only 354 days long, except for leap years, which have 355 days.

Most scientists think the Moon was formed billions of years ago by a collision between Earth and another large body. They think debris blasted into space and gradually clumped together, because of its gravitational pull, creating the Moon.

Top: The body slamming into Earth breaks up into pieces.

Bottom: The body blasts material from Earth's outer layer into space.

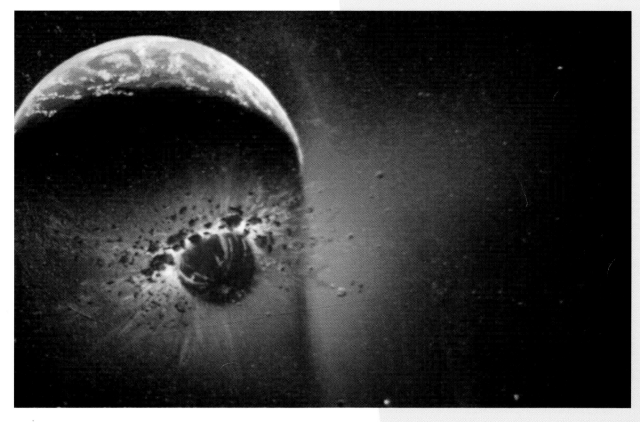

A Different World

Is there any chance that people might one day live and work on the Moon? Living on the Moon would be quite different from living on Earth. The Moon's surface gravity is only 1/6 that of Earth. It has no air for you to breathe. The Moon turns so slowly that each day and each night is two weeks long. During the day, the temperature rises to higher than the boiling point of water. During the night, the temperature gets colder than Antarctica. Since the Moon's atmosphere is very thin, it does not filter out the radiation in sunlight, nor does it burn up meteorites that are always striking. There is also no magnetic field to turn away cosmic rays.

An artist's idea of a lunar base, where people live, work, and play as lunar residents. In this view of life on the Moon, people must live within the totally artificial environments of their buildings, vehicles, and space suits. Such a setting might help prepare future "space people" for their lives as permanent settlers of the cosmos.

A child and an adult survey the scene of this lunar base in this artist's conception. Here is where the mining of our Moon's natural resources would take place. The long instrument — measuring about 6 miles (10 km) — is called a mass driver. It would provide the boost needed to lift cargo off the Moon.

Future Site of
The Apollo Museum
COMPLETION SCHEDULED

A lunar magnetic field — yes or no?

Earth has a magnetic field but the Moon does not — that is, it lacks a global field covering its entire body. Earth has a large hot core of liquid iron that swirls as our planet rotates. This produces Earth's magnetic field. The Moon is less dense than Earth, so it may have only a small core of metal, which might not even be heavy iron.

Since the Moon is small, the core may be only partially liquid or not liquid at all. Still, Moon rocks show signs that they were affected by magnetism. Could the Moon in its early days have had a hotter center than now? Could it have had a magnetic field that would have affected its early history? Scientists are not sure.

Above: An artist's conception of a robot craft operated by a cosmic construction worker in a colony between Earth and the Moon.

Lunar Life

Living on the Moon's surface seems like it would be interesting, but it could get difficult. It might, however, be possible to live comfortably on the Moon if you stayed a few yards below the surface. There, the temperature is always mild, and you would be protected from meteorites, cosmic rays, and the Sun's radiation.

People on the Moon could do valuable work setting up mining stations. The Moon's surface could yield all the construction metals. Construction parts could be easily fired into space from the Moon because of the Moon's low gravity. These parts could be used to build places where people could live and work in space.

Left: The tubelike structures on the top of this colony (*opposite*) are what human workers would call home.

The tides — are they wearing Earth down?

The tides on Earth rise and fall, so there is friction of water against the sea bottoms. Earth's rotation is slightly slowed down by this friction. When Earth takes more time to turn on its axis, the length of our days gets longer. As the Earth spins more slowly, the Moon moves farther away.

These changes are so slow that in all history they have not been very noticeable. In very old times, however, the Moon was closer to Earth; a day was shorter; the tides were higher. How did all this affect the development of Earth and its inhabitants? The answers are not known.

A New Home Base

Someday, we may mine the Moon for building materials and energy resources. Other uses for the Moon are possible, but we must be careful not to disturb it too much. Since the early days of the Solar System, the Moon has changed less than Earth. This means we can study the first billion years of the Solar System easier on the Moon than on Earth. Also, we could set up light telescopes and radio telescopes on the far side of the Moon. There would be no Earthly lights or radio signals to interfere, so we could see farther and more clearly into deep space to learn about the very early days of the Universe. Who knows what mysteries we may uncover about our Universe now that we have walked on the Moon?

Right: Tourists have invaded this imaginary Moon beach.

Imagine what it would be like if we could look at space from a site on the Moon. The artist of this picture shows workers breaking ground for construction of a huge multiple-mirror telescope on the far side of the Moon. In the background is a radio telescope and observatories with light telescopes.

Left: An artist's idea of how lunar seas with real water might look. An artificial satellite hovers above the sea. If we could create an atmosphere like Earth's on the Moon, we could capture sunlight and turn the Moon into a tourist center. This would be fun, but scientists feel it is more important to keep the Moon much as it is. In that way, we can use it to help us better understand Earth and the cosmos.

Today, thanks to unmanned probes and piloted missions, we have seen the Moon's craters close up, as well as something never before seen by humans — the far side of the Moon, which always faces away from Earth.

On these two pages, you can examine two interesting questions about the Moon's craters: 1) How were the craters formed? 2) Why are the craters on the far side so different from the ones on the near side?

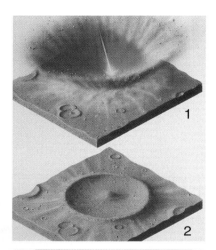

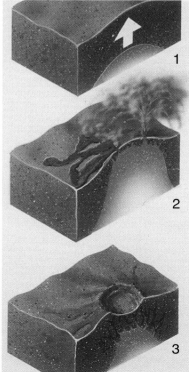

How were the Moon's craters formed?

By the Impact of Meteorites

1. A meteorite strikes the Moon's surface, sending out a shock wave that gouges a deep hole, throwing out a cone-shaped curtain of boulders and other debris that falls back to the surface.
2. The boulders create several smaller craters around the first one, and the finer debris settles into a "blanket."

Comments:
- Upon impact, the meteorite is consumed, or absorbed, into its crater.
- The matter at the center of impact "rebounds," just as a drop in a pool of water would, and freezes.
- Thin lines, or filaments, emerge as a blanket of dust settles. A pattern of lines called rays extends outward from the crater.
- Most of the Moon's craters have been formed by the impact of meteorites.

By Volcanic Action

1. A portion of the surface is forced upward by melted rock and gases from within the Moon's interior.
2. Gas and lava erput through the lunar surface and into the sky above. Pressure from below is now eased.
3. The surface collapses into a crater.

Comments:
- Volcanic craters differ from those of meteorite craters — no rays, no smaller craters nearby, and no "peak" at center of volcanic crater.
- Volcanic craters are a sign that the Moon may have once had a very active, hot inner region.
- Although virtually all the Moon's craters were formed by the impact of meteorites, some may have been formed by volcanic activity. It is unlikely there would be any current volcanic activity on the Moon — just some possible shifting or adjusting of the Moon's surface. These shifts might give rise to an occasional volcanic "burp" of trapped gas.

COMPARING CRATERS

The Near Side
vs.
The Far Side

Near Side
As these photos illustrate, the Moon's near side has fewer craters of the type found on the far side. It does have more of the maria, or seas, that appear as large dark areas. The maria are actually the result of volcanic activity that covered ancient meteorite-impact craters with flowing lava. Why did so much more volcanic activity occur on the near side, and why did so many more meteorites seem to have struck the far side? Scientists are not sure.

Far Side
Perhaps more meteor strikes occurred on the far side because Earth partly blocked the near side from meteors. Perhaps there were more volcanic eruptions on the near side because the Moon's crust is generally thinner there than on the far side. Maybe the pull of Earth's gravity on the gases and melted rock below the Moon's surface on the near side contributed to the volcanic activity. No one knows for sure.

More Books about the Moon

Apollo 11: First Moon Landing. Michael D. Cole (Enslow)

Apollo Moonwalks: The Amazing Lunar Missions. Gregory Vogt (Enslow)

Armstrong Lands on the Moon. Gordon Charleston (Dillon)

DK Space Encyclopedia. Nigel Henbest and Heather Couper (DK Publishing)

Moon Base: First Colony in Space. Michael D. Cole (Enslow)

The Moon. Carmen Bredeson (Franklin Watts)

CD-ROMs and DVDs

CD-ROM: *Exploring the Planets.* (Cinegram)

DVD: *For All Mankind: Criterion Collection.* (Home Vision Entertainment)

NASA: 25 Years of Glory. (Madacy Entertainment)

Web Sites

The Internet is a good place to get more information about the Moon. The web sites listed here can help you learn about the most recent discoveries, as well as those made in the past.

Apollo Missions. cass.jsc.nasa.gov/pub/expmoon/apollo_landings.html

Full Moon: Apollo Mission Photography. www.projectfullmoon.com/

Lunar Prospector. lunar.arc.nasa.gov/

Nine Planets. www.nineplanets.org/moon.html

Views of the Solar System. www.solarviews.com/eng/moon.htm

Windows to the Universe. www.windows.ucar.edu/tour/link=/moon/moon.html

Places to Visit

Here are some museums and centers where you can find a variety of space exhibits.

American Museum of Natural History
Central Park West at 79th Street
New York, NY 10024

Henry Crown Space Center
Museum of Science and Industry
57th Street and Lake Shore Drive
Chicago, IL 60637

National Air and Space Museum
Smithsonian Institution
7th and Independence Avenue SW
Washington, DC 20560

Odyssium
11211 142nd Street
Edmonton, Alberta T5M 4A1
Canada

Scienceworks Museum
2 Booker Street
Spotswood
Melbourne, Victoria 3015
Australia

U.S. Space and Rocket Center
1 Tranquility Base
Huntsville, AL 35807

Glossary

Armstrong, Neil: U.S. astronaut who on July 20, 1969, became the first person to step on the Moon's surface.

astronauts: men and women who travel in space.

atmosphere: the gases surrounding a planet, star, or moon. Our Moon has a very thin atmosphere containing various gases but very little oxygen.

comet: an object made of ice, rock, and gas. It has a vapor trail that can be seen when it orbits close to the Sun.

corona: the hot thin outer atmosphere of the Sun.

cosmonaut: the Russian name for astronaut.

crater: a hole or pit caused by a volcanic explosion or by the impact of a meteorite. Most craters on the Moon are due to meteorites.

eclipse: when one body crosses through the shadow of another. During a solar eclipse, parts of Earth are in the shadow of the Moon as the Moon cuts across the Sun and hides it for a period of time. A lunar eclipse occurs when the Moon is full and on the opposite side of Earth from the Sun and then passes through Earth's shadow.

full Moon: what we call the Moon when it is on the opposite side of Earth from the Sun, and its face seems fully lit.

Galileo: an Italian scientist who made a telescope through which the first clear view of the Moon's surface was seen, in 1609.

gibbous: the Moon when more than half, but not all, of its face is lit.

gravity: the force that causes objects like Earth and the Moon to be attracted to one another.

Luna 2: the first spacecraft to land on the Moon. It was launched by the former Soviet Union in 1959.

lunar: having to do with the Moon.

lunar year: the basis for ancient calendars. In a lunar year there are twelve new Moons from one spring to the next.

maria: flat, dark areas on the Moon that were once thought to contain water. The name comes from the Latin word for "seas." The dark areas were actually caused by volcanic eruptions that produced lava flows.

Moon: Earth's only satellite. It is about 238,900 miles (384,400 km) from Earth.

orbit: the path that one celestial object follows as it circles, or revolves around, another.

phases: the different ways in which the Moon's face is lit by the Sun. It takes about a month to go from full Moon to full Moon.

Pluto-Charon: the combination of planet and moon that is the nearest thing in our Solar System to a double planet. Some astronomers think that Pluto and Charon may even share the same atmosphere.

radio telescope: an instrument that uses a radio receiver and antenna to both see into space and listen for messages from space.

satellite: a small body in space that moves in an orbit around a larger body. Natural satellites are often called moons.

seas: also maria, a name used for the flat dark areas on the Moon even though they are completely waterless.

Solar System: the Sun with the planets and all the other bodies, such as the asteroids, that orbit the Sun.

Sun: our star and the provider of the energy that makes life possible on Earth.

Index

Aldrin, Edwin "Buzz" 15
Apollo spacecrafts 6-7, 13, 14, 15, 16, 18-19
Armstrong, Neil 15
atmosphere 6, 22, 26

Bean, Alan L. 15

calendar 9, 20
Charon 13
Clementine 16
comets 4
Conrad, Charles, Jr. 15
corona 11
cosmic rays 22, 25
craters 6-7, 14, 19, 28-29

daguerreotype 5
double planets 12-13

Easter 20
eclipses
    lunar 10-11
    solar 10-11

Galileo (man) 6-7
Galileo (probe) 12, 16-17
gravity and gravitational pull 4, 9, 19, 21

International Astronomical Union Crater No. 221 14
Irwin, Jim 15

Jupiter 12, 16

Langrenus (crater) 7
Luna spacecrafts 14, 16
lunar dust 18
lunar eclipse 10-11
Lunar Prospector 16

lunar soil 15, 18-19, 24
lunar time 20

magnetic field 22-23
"man in the Moon" 4-5
Mare Moscoviense 14
maria 6, 14, 19, 29
Mars 16, 20
meteorites and meteors 6, 22, 25, 28-29
moon rocks 15, 17, 19, 20
Moscow 14
Muslims 20

phases of Moon 8-9
Pluto 13

Russia 14-15

Saturn 12
seas 26
    See also maria
solar eclipse 10-11
Solar System 12, 13, 26
Soviet Union (former) 14, 15, 19
Sun 4-5, 8, 9, 10-11, 22, 25, 26

telescopes 5, 6-7, 26, 27
tides 4, 9, 25

United States 14, 15, 16, 19, 26, 27

Venus 16
volcanoes 28-29

Born in 1920, Isaac Asimov came to the United States as a young boy from his native Russia. As a young man, he was a student of biochemistry. In time, he became one of the most productive writers the world has ever known. His books cover a spectrum of topics, including science, history, language theory, fantasy, and science fiction. His brilliant imagination gained him the respect and admiration of adults and children alike. Sadly, Isaac Asimov died shortly after the publication of the first edition of *Isaac Asimov's Library of the Universe.*

The publishers wish to thank the following for permission to reproduce copyright material: front cover, 3, 20, NASA Goddard Space Flight Center; 4, © Sally Bensusen 1988; 5 (upper), Harvard College Observatory; 5 (lower), © Sally Bensusen 1988; 6, © National Geographic, Jean-Leon Huens; 7 (upper), © Dennis Milon; 7 (lower), NASA; 8 (upper), © Tom Miller 1988; 8 (lower), Lick Observatory; 9, © Tom Miller 1988; 10 (both), © Sally Bensusen 1988; 11 (both), © George East; 12, NASA/JPL; 13, NASA; 14 (upper), Oberg Archives; 14 (lower left and right), 15 (all), 16 (both), NASA; 17, NASA/JPL; 18 (upper), © William K. Hartmann; 18 (lower), 19, NASA; 21 (upper), © Ron Miller; 21 (lower), © William K. Hartmann; 22, © Mark Paternostro 1978; 22-23, Lunar & Planetary Institute © 1985, Pat Rawlings; 24, 25 © Doug McLeod 1988; 26, © David Hardy; 26-27, © Paul DiMare 1986; 27 (lower), 28 (both), © Garret Moore 1987; 29 (upper), Lick Observatory; 29 (lower), NASA.